INSPIRING ARTISTS

CLAUDE MONET

First published in Great Britain in 2016 by
The Watts Publishing Group

Copyright © 2016 The Watts Publishing Group

All rights reserved.

Editor: Julia Bird
Design: Mark Ruffle/www.rufflebrothers.co.uk
Page layout: sprout.uk.com

ISBN 978 1 4451 4561 7

Dewey number: 750

Printed in China

Franklin Watts
An imprint of
Hachette Children's Group
Part of The Watts Publishing Group
Carmelite House
50 Victoria Embankment
London EC4Y 0DZ

An Hachette UK Company
www.hachette.co.uk

www.franklinwatts.co.uk

MIX
Paper from
responsible sources
FSC® C104740

INSPIRING ARTISTS
CLauDE MONET

SUSIE BROOKS

W
FRANKLIN WATTS
LONDON • SYDNEY

Picture acknowledgements: Front cover; 3, 36; Waterlily Pond, 1899. W.C.Osborn Collection. AKG Images. Oil on canvas, 90.5 x 89.7 cm. 6l; Self-Portrait in his Atelier, c. 1884. Musée Marmottan, Paris. Oil on canvas, 54 x 85 cm. 6r; Caricature of Henri Cassinelli (Rufus Croutineli), c.1858. Art Institute of Chicago. Graphite on card, 13 x 8.5 cm. 7, 46; The Cliff Walk at Pourville, 1882. Art Institute of Chicago. Oil on canvas, 66.5 x 82.3 cm. 8t; Eugène Boudin, Low Tide, Shore and Fishermen at Sunset, 1862. Christies Images/Superstock. Oil on panel, 17.5 x 25 cm. 8b; View at Rouelles, Le Havre, 1858. Private Collection. Oil on canvas, 46 x 65 cm. 9t; Jean-François Millet, The Gleaners, 1857. Musée D'Orsay, Paris. Oil on canvas, 83.8 x 111.8 cm. 9b; Rue de la Bavole, Honfleur, 1864. Museum of Fine Art, Boston. Bequest of John T Spaulding. Oil on canvas, 55.9 x 61 cm. 10; The Woman in a Green Dress, (Camille), 1866. Kunsthalle Bremen. Oil on canvas, 231 x 151 cm. 11t; Edouard Manet, Le Déjeuner sur l'Herbe, 1862-3. Musée D'Orsay, Paris. Oil on canvas, 208 x 265.5 cm. 11b; Women in the Garden, 1866. Musée D'Orsay, Paris. Oil on canvas, 255 x 205 cm. 12b & 12t detail; Bathers at Grenouillère, 1869. National Gallery, London. Bridgeman Art Library/Superstock. Oil on canvas, 73 x 92 cm. 13t; Pierre-Auguste Renoir, La Grenouillère, 1869. Pushkin Museum of Fine Arts, Moscow. Superstock. Oil on canvas, 80 x 59cm. 13b; Impression, Sunrise, 1872. Musée Marmottan, Paris. Oil on canvas, 48 x 63 cm. 14; Beach at Trouville, 1870. National Gallery, London. D'Agostini/Superstock. Oil on canvas, 38 x 46.5 cm. 15t; Edouard Manet, Monet in his Studio Boat, 1874. Neue Pinakothek, Munich. Oil on canvas, 82.5 x 105 cm. 15b; Regatta at Argenteuil, 1872. Musée D'Orsay, Paris. Peter Willi/Superstock. Oil on canvas, 48 x 75 cm. 16t; Utagawa Hiroshige, Driving Rain at Shono, c.1833. Edo Tokyo Museum. Colour woodblock print, 22.6 x 34.8 cm. 16b; Katsushika Hokusai, View of the Pontoon Bridge at Sano, 1834. Minneapolis Institute of Art. Colour woodblock print, 25.5 x 37.1 cm. 17; View of Argenteuil in the Snow, 1875. Nelson Atkins Museum of Art, Kansas City. Album/Prisma/Superstock. Oil on canvas, 54 x 65 cm. 18bl; Boulevard des Capucines, 1873. Nelson Atkins Museum of Art, Kansas City. Oil on canvas, 80.3 x 60.3 cm. 18tr & 18c detail; Rue Montorgueil, Paris. Festival of 30 June, 1878. Musée D'Orsay, Paris. Bridgeman Art Library/Superstock. Oil on canvas, 81 x 50 cm. 19; Robert Delaunay, Red Eiffel Tower, 1911-12. Solomon R Guggenheim Museum, New York. Bridgeman Art Library. Oil on canvas, 125 x 90 cm. 20; Train in the Snow, 1875. Musée Marmottan, Paris. Peter Willi/Superstock. Oil on canvas, 59 x 78 cm. 21t; La Gare Saint-Lazare, 1877 Musée D'Orsay, Paris. Oil on canvas, 74 x 104 cm. 21b; Joseph Mallord William Turner, Rain, Steam and Speed - The Great Western Railway, 1844. National Gallery, London. Fine Art Images/Superstock. Oil on canvas, 91 x 121.8 cm. 22t; View of Vetheuil, Path in the Ile Saint-Martin, 1880. Metropolitan Museum of Art, New York. Oil on canvas, 80 x 60.3 cm. 22b; Vetheuil in the Mist, 1879. Musée Marmottan, Paris. Bridgeman Art Library. Oil on canvas, 60 x 71 cm. 23; Paul Cézanne, L'Estaque with Red Roofs, 1883-85. Private Collection. Oil on canvas, 65 x 81 cm. 24; Etretat, Rough Sea, 1883. Musée des Beaux- Arts, Lyon. Giraudon/Bridgeman Art Library. Oil on canvas, 100 x 81 cm. 25t; Etretat in the Rain, 1886. National Gallery Oslo. O. Vaering/Bridgeman Art Library. Oil on canvas, 60.5 x 73.5 cm. 25b: Vincent van Gogh, Seascape at Saintes-Maries (Fishing Boats at Sea) 1888. Pushkin Museum of Fine Arts, Moscow. Oil on canvas, 44 x 53 cm. 26r & 26cl detail; Woman with Parasol (Study of a Figure Outdoors, Facing Left), 1886. Musée D'Orsay, Paris. Album/Joseph Martin/Superstock. Oil on canvas, 131 x 88 cm. 27t & 27b detail; Georges Seurat, Sunday Afternoon on the Island of La Grande Jatte, 1884-6. Art Institute of Chicago. Oil on canvas, 207.5 x 308.1 cm. 28; Morning at Antibes, 1888. Philadelphia Museum of Art. Oil on canvas, 65.7 x 82.1 cm. 29t; Antibes, Afternoon Effect, 1888. Museum of Fine art, Boston. Oil on canvas, 66 x 82.5 cm. 29b; André Derain, Boats in the Harbour at Collioure, 1905. Private Collection. © ADAGP, Paris and DACS, London 2015. Bridgeman Art Library. Oil on canvas, 72 x 91 cm. 30, 47t ; Haystacks at End of Summer, Morning Effect, 1891. Musée D'Orsay. Paris. Oil on canvas, 60.5 x 100.8 cm. 31t; Haystacks, Snow Effect, Morning, 1891. J. Paul Getty Museum, Malibu. Oil on canvas, 64.8 x 99.7 cm. 31b; Wassily Kandinsky, Composition IV, 1911. Kunstsammlung Nordrhein-Westfalen, Dusseldorf. Oil on canvas, 159.5 x 250.5 cm. 32bl, 47b; Rouen Cathedral, West Façade, Sunlight, 1894. National Gallery of Art, Washington. Oil on canvas, 100.1 x 65.8 cm. 32br; Rouen Cathedral in the Fog, 1894. Private Collection. Oil on canvas, 106 x 73 cm. 33t; Roy Lichtenstein, Rouen Cathedral, Set V, 1968-9. © Estate of Roy Lichtenstein/DACS 2015. Anderson Collection/SFMOMA. Oil and magna on canvas, 161.61 x 360.36 cm. 33b; Rouen Cathedral, Sun Effect, End of Day, 1892-3. Musée Marmottan, Paris. Oil on canvas, 100 x 65 cm. 34; Houses of Parliament, Effect of Sunlight in the Fog, 1904. Musée D'Orsay, Paris. Bridgeman Art Library. Oil on canvas, 81 x 92 cm. 35t; James Abbott McNeil Whistler, Nocturne: Blue and Silver-Chelsea, 1871. Tate Britain, London. Oil on wood, 60.8 x 50.2 cm. 35b; Waterloo Bridge, c. 1901. Private Collection. Pastel on paper, 31 x 48.5 cm. 37t; Water Lilies, 1906. Art Institute of Chicago. Fine Art/Alamy. Oil on canvas, 89.9 x 94.1 cm. 37b; Andy Warhol, Flowers, 1964. Private Collection. © 2015 The Andy Warhol Foundation for the Visual Arts, Inc./Artists Rights Society (ARS), New York and DACS, London. Christies Images/Superstock. Acrylic, silkscreen ink and pencil on linen, 205.4 x205.7 cm. 38t; Monet at work in 1923 at Giverny. Hulton Archive/Getty Images. 38b; Morning with Weeping Willows, 1926. Musée de l'Orangerie, Paris. Superstock. Oil on canvas, 200 x 425 cm. 39t; Musée de l'Orangerie, Paris, interior with Water Lilies. Jacques Demarthon/AFP/Getty Images. 39b; Pierre Bonnard, Landscape in the South (Le Cannet), 1943. Metropolitan Museum of Art, New York. © ADAGP, Paris and DACS, London 2015. Art Resource, New York/Scala, Florence. Oil on canvas, 64.1 x 71.1 cm. 40l & 40r detail; The Artists' House seen from the Rose Garden, 1922. Musée Marmottan, Paris. AKG Images. Oil on canvas, 89 x 92 cm. 41t; The Japanese Bridge at Giverny, 1918–1924. Musée Marmottan, Paris. Bridgeman Art Library. Oil on canvas, 89 x 116 cm. 41b; Jackson Pollock, Reflection of the Big Dipper, 1946. Stedelijk Museum, Amsterdam. © The Pollock-Krasner Foundation ARS, NY and DACS, London 2015. Stedelijk Museum Amsterdam/Getty Images. Oil on canvas, 111 x 91.5 cm. 42; Water Lilies and Reflections of a Willow Tree, 1916-1919. Musée Marmottan, Paris. Bridgeman Art Library. Oil on canvas, 200 x 200 cm. 43t; Childe Hassan, Men o'War: 'The Blake' and 'The Boston', 1893. Private Collection. Oil on canvas. 45.7 x 56.5 cm. 43b; Joan Mitchell, La Grande Vallée XVI, Pour Iva, 1983. © Estate of Joan Mitchell. Courtesy of the Joan Mitchell Foundation, New York. Oil on canvas, 259.715 x 199.707 cm.

CONTENTS

A NATURAL ARTIST

Monet captured the world differently from artists who had come before him. He painted with quick, unblended brushstrokes and daring colours. At first people criticised his bright, dappled paintings – but that didn't stop them becoming some of the best-loved images in art history.

Self Portrait in his Atelier, c.1884

Caricature of Henri Cassinelli (Rufus Croutinelli), c.1858

INSPIRING TIMES

Oscar-Claude Monet was born in Paris, France, in 1840. His father was a grocer and his mother a singer, and while Monet was still a boy his family moved north to the Normandy coast. Monet would rush to the beach in all weathers, setting the scene for a love of nature that would later show in his work. The modernising world around him had an impact on his future painting too. Monet's artistic talent began to show at school, where he drew caricatures of his teachers (as above). By the age of 15 he was earning money from these cheeky portraits! His father wanted him to go into business, but his mother encouraged his art.

The Cliff Walk at Pourville, 1882

WORKING OUTDOORS

Monet always enjoyed sketching outdoors, and working in the open air became the key to his famous style. He took his easel out into fields or to the seaside, painting scenes like the one above. Most of all, Monet wanted to capture the effects of natural light on the world around him. He was intrigued by the colours and atmospheres that changed throughout the day and in different weathers and seasons. He found a new way to show them, using swift, broken brushstrokes and bright, vibrant shades of paint.

GREAT IMPRESSIONS

Monet's style became known as Impressionism – which at first was meant as an insult. People said his works were sketchy and unfinished. But in his lifetime Monet achieved huge success and inspired many other artists. He created a turning point in painting and showed that colour could be used in a brand new way (see p.13). Generations of painters, from Georges Seurat (1859–1891) (see p.26–27) to Joan Mitchell (1925–1992) (see p.43), benefited from this – and artists still feel Monet's influence today.

PLEIN-AIR PAINTING

Monet was introduced to painting by the landscape artist Eugène Boudin (1824–1898), who had spotted the skill in the teenager's caricatures. Monet didn't think much of Boudin's work at first, but he agreed to paint with him outdoors. This opened up a whole new world for Monet – one he would hold onto for most of his career.

OUT AND ABOUT

Monet and Boudin painted by the sea and in the countryside around their local area, Le Havre (right). Although sketching in the open air (or *plein air*) was nothing new in the 19th century, outdoor oil painting was greatly helped by the invention of squeezable paint tubes in 1841. These were easy to carry and stopped the paint from drying out, unlike the pigs' bladders that artists had stored their paint in before.

LOOKING AT LIGHT

Boudin encouraged his young friend to look at the effects of light on the landscape. Monet later said the experience was like a veil being lifted before his eyes. His early work, such as *View at Rouelles, Le Havre* (below, right), shows strong sunlight and shadows, blue skies and drifting clouds. There are flickers of sketchy brushstrokes, but also a solid sense of space that links it to traditional art.

'I want to show you Honfleur; I want you to see the light.' –Boudin to Monet

Low Tide – Shore and Fishermen at Sunset, Eugène Boudin, 1862

OUTSIDE PARIS

In 1859, Monet moved to Paris to study painting. Here he was influenced by other artists, including Gustave Courbet (1819–1877) and Jean-François Millet (1814–1875), who were venturing out of the city to work from nature. They also painted scenes of everyday rural life, such as *The Gleaners* (opposite, top). This was relatively rare in art before their time.

View at Rouelles, Le Havre, 1858

The Gleaners, Jean-François Millet, 1857

AFRICAN HEAT

Monet had a break from Paris in 1861, when he was called for military service. He ended up in Algeria, northern Africa, then part of the French Republic. There he marvelled at the intense, sunlit colours of the landscape. The following year he came home after catching typhoid – but his African experience soon filtered into his work. You can see it in the vivid colours and sense of heat and shade in *Rue de la Bavole, Honfleur* (right). This coastal town was a popular place for painters, with its bright weather and pretty streets. Monet captured a moment in autumn when the afternoon sun was starting to go down.

Rue de la Bavole, Honfleur, 1864

MODELS IN A GARDEN

When artists wanted to paint people, they would usually pose models in a studio where it was easy to control the lighting. Monet learned to work in this way when he moved to Paris for his art training. But he also did something revolutionary – posing figures outside, in natural light.

SALON SUBJECTS

The best way for artists of Monet's day to get recognised was to show their work at the Salon – an annual art exhibition in Paris. The Salon favoured traditional subjects such as historical, biblical or mythological scenes. Artists like Monet, with different ideas, rarely fitted the bill.

ACCEPTED WORK

The Salon accepted a degree of innovation, and they selected Monet's *The Woman in a Green Dress* (left) for the 1866 show. Monet painted it from life in a studio and made the figure and her rich clothing look real. Unconventionally, he captured a moment of movement from behind, rather than showing a still, frontal portrait pose. The model is Camille Doncieux, who later became Monet's wife.

INSPIRED BY MANET

French artist Edouard Manet (1832–1883) painted *Le Déjeuner sur l'Herbe* (opposite, top), which was rejected by the Salon of 1863. This painting caused shockwaves in official circles and attracted a lot of attention. For a start, it showed a naked woman picnicking with men in modern clothes. Before this, the only nudes painted in a landscape were characters from myths or the Bible. Manet's colours were radical, with stark darks and lights, and he avoided perspective – the way artists traditionally show depth in a scene. All this inspired Monet to try his own version.

The Woman in a Green Dress (also known as *Camille*), 1866

Le Déjeuner sur l'Herbe, Edouard Manet, 1862–1863

POSING OUTDOORS

Manet's work was posed in a studio, but Monet didn't like artificial light – he sketched outside, then started on a huge final canvas back indoors. He never finished it, but soon went a step further and painted a whole posed scene outdoors. *Women in the Garden* was so big (over 2.5 metres in height) that Monet dug a trench in the ground so he could reach every part! Painting a humble, everyday subject on this scale was very new. Doing it outdoors was a first.

 **ART SPOT** *Women in the Garden is a study of light rather than people. What do you notice about the figures? Is there any sense of story? Why do you think the Salon rejected this work?*

Women in the Garden, 1866

FIRST IMPRESSIONS

During his time in Paris, Monet made friends with other up-and-coming artists, including Pierre-Auguste Renoir (1841–1919) and Alfred Sisley (1839–1899). They gathered in cafés to discuss ideas and made trips to paint *en plein air*. Together they forged a movement that became known as Impressionism.

FLEETING EFFECTS

The next time you are outside, notice how a view can change in a moment with the passing of a cloud or a gust of wind. Monet and his friends wanted to capture these fleeting effects. They did it by painting quick, visible brushstrokes that make the picture look spontaneous. It gives the *impression* of flickering light, rippling reflections and

movement. You can see this in the paintings on these pages – *Bathers at La Grenouillère* (below) was one of Monet's earliest works in this style, and may have been a sketch for a larger canvas.

ART SPOT *Notice how Monet reduced his figures to just a few slabs of paint. The swimmers in the water are shown as disjointed blobs. What effect does this have?*

Bathers at La Grenouillère, 1869

PURE COLOUR

The way the artists used colour in these paintings was ground-breaking. Traditionally painters mixed and blended their shades across the canvas, but Monet and his friends placed streaks of pure colour alongside each other (see p.15). Sometimes they would apply paint straight from the tube, rather than using a brush. This means that close-up the pictures can be hard to read, but further back they come into focus.

NEW NICKNAME

Such 'unpolished' paintings were baffling to people of Monet's day. They were nothing like the slick works shown at the Salon. Eventually, in 1874, Monet's group put together their own exhibition. When the art critic Louis Leroy saw Monet's *Impression, Sunrise*, (below) he said it was like a sketch for a wallpaper pattern – this wasn't meant as a compliment! He nicknamed the group 'the Impressionists', and after a while the name stuck.

La Grenouillère, Pierre-Auguste Renoir, 1869

 ART SPOT *Renoir loved to paint people out enjoying themselves. What differences do you notice between the above painting and Monet's? Look at the brushwork as well as what's in the scene.*

Impression, Sunrise, 1872

BEACHES AND BOATS

Coasts and rivers fascinated Monet from his early days. He was drawn by the sea breeze, the shifting shadows and especially the glimmer of sunlight on water. Working on small canvases that he could easily carry around, he tried to paint what he saw and experienced at instant points in time.

SUMMER DAYS

Monet painted *Beach at Trouville* (below) on his honeymoon, having married Camille. The pair had stopped at the northern French coast on their way to England to escape the Franco-Prussian War (1870–1871). We can tell this picture was made outside, because grains of sand are mingled with the paint. A flash of harsh sunlight is caught on Camille's skirt, while the umbrella casts a shadow on her face.

ART SPOT *Monet painted* Beach at Trouville *in a single sitting. The quick brushwork makes it seem immediate, like a snapshot. How does the composition (layout) of the painting add to this effect?*

Beach at Trouville, 1870

JUST A GLIMPSE

Monet left patches of the primed canvas bare in *Beach at Trouville* – look at the hand of the lady on the right of the painting, for example. Her face seems incomplete too, shown with just a few marks. It gives us a sense of how the human eye works – when we glimpse a scene, we don't see everything at once in detailed focus.

Monet in his Studio Boat, Edouard Manet, 1874

ON THE RIVER

In 1871, Monet moved to the suburb of Argenteuil, outside Paris. Here the River Seine captured his attention – so much so that he converted a boat into a floating studio! You can see him at work on it, accompanied by Camille, in Edouard Manet's painting *Monet in his Studio Boat* (above). *Regatta at Argenteuil* (below) shows Monet's skill at depicting reflections. Here he used complementary colours with maximum contrast, including blue/orange and red/green. He knew that placing these colours next to each other would make them look extra vibrant.

COLOUR SCIENCE

The Impressionists learned a lot from 19th century scientists, who were working out how different colours affected each other. Monet and friends rejected pure black, mixing dark tones instead from combinations of complementary colours. Their shadows were often blue or purple, in contrast to golden sunlight. They also had access to a new range of synthetic pigments – vivid colours such as chrome yellows and cobalt blue that were not seen in earlier art.

Regatta at Argenteuil, 1872

EASTERN INFLUENCE

From the 1860s, a new wave of influence began to hit French artists – all the way from the Far East. Japan had recently opened its ports to trade with Europe, and a flood of items, including Japanese prints, arrived in Paris. Monet was one of many people who joined the craze that was named 'Japonisme'.

DECORATIVE STYLE

Japanese printmakers such as Katsushika Hokusai (1760–1849) and Utagawa Hiroshige (1797–1858) turned everyday life and the changing weather into decorative works of art.

Shōno – Driving Rain, Katsushika Hiroshige, c.1833

View of the Pontoon Bridge at Sano, Utagawa Hokusai, 1834

Naturally this appealed to the Impressionists. What also appealed were the Japanese artists' bold colours and quirky compositions, where the subject was often off-centre or cropped at the picture edge. In the prints on the opposite page, *Shōno – Driving Rain* and *View of the Pontoon Bridge at Sano*, you can see how Hiroshige and Hokusai focused more on overall design than on realistic detail. Monet enjoyed all aspects of these works. He collected over 200 Japanese prints in his lifetime.

INSPIRED DESIGN

In Monet's *View of Argenteuil in the Snow* (below), Japanese influence can be seen in the simple shapes of figures carrying umbrellas and elsewhere. The path trails off in a diagonal line, trees are cropped in the foreground, and the colours are heightened. Like Japanese artists, Monet reminds us that we're looking at a picture, not the real world. The two-dimensional surface of the canvas is as important as the three-dimensional scene it shows.

ART SPOT *Notice Monet's use of blues and purples in the shadows. How does his colouring compare to the Japanese prints? What other similarities and differences can you spot?*

View of Argenteuil in the Snow, 1875

CITY SNAPSHOTS

Paris had a major facelift in the second half of the 19th century. Monet and his contemporaries were impressed by the elegant new boulevards, buzzing with modern life. Using their rapid brushstrokes and choosing radical viewpoints, they captured the dynamism of this fast-changing capital city.

PHOTO FINISH

The first Impressionist exhibition (see p.13) was held at the upper-storey studio of a photographer called Nadar. Monet painted *Boulevard des Capucines* (below) from this studio. You can see the influence of photography in the figures and carriages which look blurred, like a snapshot of something moving. The camera was a recent invention in Monet's day – it helped artists to study movement and experiment with different angles and compositions. Nadar had taken some photographs of Paris from a hot-air balloon, showing people a new view of the city.

Boulevard des Capucines, 1873

Rue Montorgueil in Paris, Festival of 30 June, 1878

ART SPOT *The French flag has three coloured stripes: red, white and blue. What do you notice about the way Monet painted the flags here?*

18

Red Eiffel Tower,
Robert Delaunay,
1911–12

DISSOLVED FORMS

You can almost hear the noise from the street in
Monet's *Rue Montorgueil in Paris, Festival of 30
June* (opposite, top). The swarming crowds and
flapping flags suggest a flurry of excitement.
The picture shows space through traditional
perspective, where the buildings converge and
look smaller towards the distance – but there
are no solid lines or fiddly details. Up close,
everything dissolves into dashes of colour.
You have to step back for the picture to
become clear.

MODERN PROGRESS

Like Monet, many other artists born in the
19th century were inspired by the thrill of the
modern world. Robert Delaunay (1885–1941)
chose to paint the famous Eiffel Tower, a radio
tower originally built for the 1889 World's Fair
in Paris. He blasted this symbol of progress
into an explosion of shapes that make it look
almost like a space rocket. In all, he painted
the Eiffel Tower over 30 times. This painting is
characteristic of a later art style called Cubism,
though Delaunay owed his bright colours to
Monet's group.

RAIL AND STEAM

Few symbols of the modern age gripped Monet as much as steam trains. France was extending its railways, and noisy, grimy locomotives were chugging to and fro. Monet loved the way the puffing steam blurred and muffled the shapes of things. He often set up his easel at stations or alongside railway tracks.

FAST AND FLEETING

Living in Argenteuil, Monet observed how nature and modern engineering met. He painted landscapes with engines barging through them, such as *Train in the Snow* (below), or bridges towering above.

Trains weren't generally seen as worthy art subjects or pleasing to look at in those days – but their speed and steam embodied the idea of constant change that Monet wanted to paint.

STATION SERIES

In 1877, Monet rented an apartment in Paris close to the Gare Saint-Lazare. He made such an impression at the station that they even held up trains while he worked! Railway workers cleared platforms and kept the engines stoked with coal, to puff out all the steam Monet wanted. He painted 12 different views here, concocting the grime from a rainbow of colours instead of blacks and greys (opposite, top).

Train in the Snow, 1875

The Gare Saint-Lazare, 1877

Rain, Steam, and Speed – the Great Western Railway,
JMW Turner, 1844

ART SPOT *Notice how the thickness of paint varies in* The Gare Saint-Lazare. *What is more important – the sunlight and steam or the solid structure of the station?*

TURNER'S TRAIN

On Monet's trip to England in 1870, he had admired the work of JMW Turner (1775–1851). This British artist was creating images of changing light and movement years before the Impressionists. His *Rain, Steam, and Speed,* (below) captures exactly what it says in the title. As in Monet's work, the train takes second place to the atmosphere, which is all about energy and the elements. Most of the canvas is covered in a mass of abstract marks.

BACK TO NATURE

At the end of the 1870s, Monet had a switch in interest – the stamps of urban life disappeared from his work and he turned his attentions back to nature. The change was mainly due to a move to the quiet village of Vétheuil on the outskirts of Paris. Here he soaked up the country air and tried to translate it into paint.

WINTER CHILL

When the Monets moved to Vétheuil with their two children, Camille was very ill. She died in 1879, just before a savage winter kicked in. Monet painted *Vétheuil in the Mist* (below) during this sad, chilly season. The distant village looks almost like a mountain range, glinting through an eerie fog. We can just make out a boat on the water, but most detail is lost in Monet's hazy mask of paint, which creates a ghostly atmosphere.

View of Vétheuil/Path in the Île Saint-Martin, 1880

Vétheuil in the Mist, 1879

SUMMER HEAT

We get a very different feel from *View of Vétheuil/Path in the Île Saint-Martin* (opposite, top) although it shows the same church in the distance. The colours are intense, with bright red poppies leaping out against their complementary colour, green. Monet designed the scene carefully – notice how the diagonals lead our eye into the distance. But at the same time it looks spontaneous, with lively brushstrokes that vary from the dappled meadow to the sweeping sky and clouds.

INDIGOMANIA

Monet once said, 'I have finally discovered the true colour of the atmosphere. It's violet. Fresh air is violet.' The Impressionists so often used shades of purple in their work that one critic accused them of having 'indigomania'. You can see flashes of it across Monet's foggy scene in *Vétheuil in the Mist* (opposite, bottom).

SOLID STYLE

Paul Cézanne (1839–1906) is known as the 'father of modern art' – but he had a lot to thank the Impressionists for. They inspired him to work outdoors and to use pure, bright colours in his work. Cézanne wanted to add something more solid to Monet's style – to show the timeless, rather than fleeting, side of nature. He tried to do this by building shapes out of blocks of colour, and keeping an ordered structure to his painting, as can be seen below in *L'Estaque with Red Roofs*. Cézanne's geometric style led to the development of Cubism (see p.19).

ART SPOT *Cézanne said, 'Monet is only an eye – but what an eye!' What do you think he meant by this? How is his painting similar to Monet's work, and how is it different?*

L'Estaque with Red Roofs, Paul Cézanne, 1883–1885

WILD WEATHER

Monet never forgot the Normandy coast of his youth, and in the 1880s he made repeated trips there. He set out to work on cliffs and beaches, happy to paint with the wind and rain beating at his beard. At one point, a wave even knocked him off a ledge and swept away his canvas and easel!

FEEL THE STORM

At this stage in his career, Monet carried several canvases with him, often using his children as porters. Juggling different paintings meant that he could stop and start on various views as the sky or weather changed. In *Etretat, Rough Sea*

Etretat, Rough Sea, 1883

(below), violent streaks of light skate across the wind-whipped waves. The atmosphere is stormy and cold – you can feel what it was like to be there. In many ways it seems more real than a photograph.

EXPRESSIVE STROKES

In the later painting *Etretat in the Rain* (opposite, top), Monet uses far less detail to describe the dramatic weather. His brushstrokes sweep back and forth, giving the impression of driving rain and wind. We can almost hear the howling gale and feel the sting of the water. Expressing an experience like this became an increasingly popular way of tackling art. Styles such as Expressionism emerged as artists began using colour and marks to convey their feelings or a particular mood.

Etretat in the Rain, 1886

MACKEREL WATER

Vincent van Gogh (1853–1890) described the colour of the sea as 'like mackerel' – in other words, like the shiny fish, it changes in different lights. He was influenced by the Impressionists and by Japanese prints, as you can see in *Seascape at Saintes-Maries* (right). Van Gogh used a more extreme form of *impasto* (thickly applied paint) than Monet. He painted at high speed and chose colours for their emotional effect. In this way his work was Expressionist.

 **ART SPOT** *Monet loved the sea so much, he said he wanted to be buried in a buoy! How did he conjure up the feeling of a storm? Look at the colours and brushstrokes.*

Seascape at Saintes-Maries (Fishing Boats at Sea),
Vincent van Gogh, 1888

FIGURES OUTDOORS

Monet occasionally painted portraits, but his figures were mostly more anonymous. He liked to show people surrounded by nature – in his garden, on boats or out in the fields. He often used his family as models. Since Camille's death he had lived with another woman, Alice Hoschedé, and her six children.

STRIKING FIGURE

Woman with a Parasol (below) was modelled by Alice's daughter, Suzanne – but we can't tell this by looking at the painting. Monet has wiped out all her facial features with the light blue wisps of a windswept veil. He chose a striking low viewpoint, as if putting her high on a pedestal. The detail is in the colours and the richly textured paint, rather than the subject itself.

ART SPOT

Monet's brushstrokes animate the figure and make her seem alive. How do the people in Seurat's Sunday Afternoon on the Island of La Grande Jatte *(opposite, top) look in comparison? Why do you think this is?*

ATTRACTING ATTENTION

Suzanne posed for another version of this painting, holding the same parasol and wearing the same dress. Monet knew that the pair of paintings looked unorthodox enough to attract attention. He was partly reacting to a ripple of new interest that was taking place in Paris. Neo-Impressionists such as Georges Seurat were borrowing the themes and colours of Monet's art, but taking them in a new direction (see opposite). Monet was a competitive man and did not want to be outdone.

Woman with a Parasol (Study of a Figure Outdoors, Facing Left), 1886

NEW IMPRESSIONS

From the early 1880s, Monet had distanced himself from the Impressionists. He was living away from Paris, the group were starting to diverge in style, and Monet was having successful exhibitions of his own. The final Impressionist show in 1886 was dominated by

Sunday Afternoon on the Island of La Grand Jatte, Georges Seurat, 1884–1886

Seurat's *Sunday Afternoon on the Island of La Grande Jatte*. It was huge and made entirely of dots of pure colour, relying on the viewer's eyes to mix them. This scientific style was known as Divisionism, or Pointillism.

 **ART SPOT** *There are more than three million dots in Seurat's painting! He used contrasting colours to make different areas stand out. Hold the page away from you. What happens to the dots?*

LIGHT AND COLOUR

Monet travelled a lot during the 1880s. During a trip to Antibes in southern France, he returned to the problem of recording changes in light and weather. Producing about 40 paintings in just four months, he grappled with the 'magical air' of the Mediterranean at different times of day.

COLOURED JEWELS

Capturing the right effect didn't come easily to Monet. He wrote to Alice: 'How beautiful it is here, to be sure, but how difficult to paint!...It's so clear and pure in its pinks and blues that the slightest misjudged stroke looks like a smear of dirt.' What he really needed on his palette, he said, were 'gold and precious stones'.

PEACEFUL MORNING

You can almost see the jewels that Monet talked about in *Morning at Antibes* (below). He built up the painting from tiny touches of colour that give the impression of shimmering light. The wafting branches of the olive tree create a frame for the distant town, which glows in the morning haze. The effect is warm and welcoming – we get the feeling of having the place all to ourselves.

HOT AFTERNOON

In *Antibes, Afternoon Effect* (opposite, top), the colours are more intense as the heat of the day builds up. Monet brings the fort of Antibes

Morning at Antibes, 1888

Antibes, Afternoon Effect, 1888

closer, gleaming in yellows and oranges against the blue-violet mountains behind. The water ripples with so much green and pink that it hints at the water lilies that he famously painted later (see p.36–39). People loved the decorative effect of these Antibes pictures, and Monet's work shot up in value as he became a household name.

BLAZING BOATS

André Derain (1880–1954) was also struck by the dazzling light of the Mediterranean. He inherited the ideas of both Monet and Seurat (see p.27), but he fired them to a whole new level. His blazing red beach, the green layer of sky and the hot-pink mountains do not reflect the real world – but they do generate an atmosphere. Derain and others who painted in this extreme style were nicknamed the 'Fauves', or 'wild beasts'.

Boats in the Harbour at Collioure, André Derain, 1905

PAINTING THE IMPOSSIBLE

Light and air became so important to Monet that he began to see them as the subject of his art. 'Other painters paint a bridge, a house, a boat,' he said. 'I want to paint the air in which the bridge, the house and the boat are to be found.' He declared that this was impossible – but even so, he set out to do it!

SERIES START

Monet had long been interested in showing the changing conditions of nature. What was different in his *Haystacks* pictures was the way he went about it. Instead of painting scenic landscapes or any other familiar art subject, he took the simple shape of a stack of grain – and painted it over and over again. He created the first of what have now become known as his series paintings.

Haystacks at End of Summer, Morning Effect, 1891

LIGHT ENVELOPE

The *Haystacks* are all about effects and sensations as opposed to actual objects. Monet was intent on showing what he called the *'enveloppe'* of light and atmosphere that surrounds things. He would hover around the haystacks at any time of day and in all seasons, flitting from one canvas to the next and cataloguing the passing of time. When he had painted what he could outdoors, he would return to his studio and complete the pictures, so that each one balanced with the next. In the painting below we see light, summery colours as the sun rises to warm the day. It contrasts with the sun on snow (opposite, top).

SHOW SUCCESS

In 1891, Monet exhibited a set of 15 haystacks paintings, hung in a row in a single room in Paris. Displaying a single-subject series like this had never been done before. The show was a gigantic hit.

Haystacks, Snow Effect, Morning, 1891

ABSTRACT BEGINNINGS

When the Russian artist Wassily Kandinsky (1866–1944) first saw Monet's *Haystacks* in a Moscow museum, he was shocked by the lack of subject. He had to check the catalogue to find out what he was looking at! Then he realised that it wasn't the objects themselves that mattered, but the colour and the paint. Taking this on board, he went on to produce some of the first truly abstract art. His work focused on mood or feeling, rather than tangible objects. The impact of paintings such as *Composition IV* (below) comes from their colours and shapes.

ART SPOT *This painting isn't fully abstract as there are still some recognisable features. Can you make out two figures and a castle on a hilltop? What else do you see here?*

Composition IV,
Wassily Kandinsky, 1911

SUNLIT STONE

It wasn't long before Monet turned his attention to a new subject – Rouen Cathedral. He set up a studio above a shop opposite the cathedral and worked repeatedly on up to 14 canvases a day. Getting to grips with this theme proved tricky, and Monet spent several years trying to perfect his work.

NO LINES

Monet painted about 30 versions of the cathedral, from three or four different nearby positions. He called it 'an immense task'. You can see from these paintings how he tried to show the building's structure without using lines. Monet persistently played down the importance of drawing, though actually he filled sketchbooks with skilled pencil work. His Rouen paintings are all about colour and texture – some critics compared the crusty paint to carved stone itself.

WORKING PROCESS

The unfinished *Rouen Cathedral, Sun Effect, End of the Day* (opposite, bottom) gives us clues about how Monet worked. He began with layers of much thinner paint before building up the impasto. Look at the sky where it meets the cathedral – there's a lighter blue beneath. Monet darkened it to contrast with the pale golden tones of the portal, and to balance the shadow that floods the bottom of the scene.

Rouen Cathedral, the Portal in the Sun, 1894

Rouen Cathedral in the Fog, 1894

Rouen Cathedral, Set V, Roy Lichtenstein, 1968–1969

MANUFACTURED MONET

In the 1960s, more than 60 years after Monet's Rouen, the US Pop Artist Roy Lichtenstein (1923–1997) produced his own cathedral series. He called the pictures 'manufactured Monets', because they imitated the earlier artist's work in a modern, mechanical style. Lichtenstein recreated the Ben-Day dots used in comic-book printing by painting through holes in a stencil. He was commenting on the way Monet's images had become so famous that they were being reproduced in endless books and prints.

ART SPOT *Lichtenstein's colours produce different effects, just as Monet's did. What time of day or type of weather would you link to each of the cathedrals above?*

Rouen Cathedral, Sun Effect, End of the Day, 1892–1893

ARTIST ON TOUR

Monet's travel itch remained in his later life and took him on trips to Norway, London and Venice from the late 1890s. What he loved about London was the fog. He had painted it during a stay there some 30 years before (see p.14), and was ready to revisit the theme of misty views over the River Thames.

CHANGING VIEW

Monet took a room at the Savoy Hotel, where he could see panoramic views of the river and the Houses of Parliament from the balcony. He soon had dozens of canvases underway, because the mists changed so quickly that he had to start afresh to show each new effect.

He began almost 100 works in London around this time, and took them back to France to complete in his studio.

FIERY FOG

As ever, Monet focused on atmosphere. Look at the brushstrokes in *Houses of Parliament, Effect of Sunlight in the Fog* (below) – they float horizontally in the water, then rise in diagonals to merge with the vertical marks of the buildings. This gives a sense of drifting fog, which continues to swirl in the sky. Meanwhile, a sizzling sun scorches through and lights a fiery beam across the river. The overall effect is mysterious and dreamlike.

Houses of Parliament, Effect of Sunlight in the Fog, 1904

Nocturne: Blue and Silver – Chelsea,
James Abbott McNeill Whistler, 1871

PASTEL SKETCHES

On one of his journeys to London, Monet's paints got held up at customs. Annoyed at the delay to his work, he went to buy some pastels from an art shop. This view of Waterloo Bridge (below, right) is one of 26 pastel drawings he made at the time. He soon turned back to painting, but wrote to Alice: 'It is thanks to my pastels, made swiftly, that I realised how to proceed.'

ART SPOT *Monet smudged the chalky pastels with his finger to create a delicate misty effect. Can you see how this affected his painting?*

MOONLIT RIVER

Another artist who painted ethereal views of the Thames was James McNeill Whistler (1834–1903). This eccentric American was a great friend of Monet's and shared a keen interest in Turner's work (see p.21). Whistler wanted to capture the tranquility of the river in his moonlit scenes, or 'nocturnes'. His simplified shapes and whispers of colour create an atmospheric feel like Monet's.

Waterloo Bridge, 1901

A GLORIOUS GARDEN

Monet had bought a house in the village of Giverny, northwest of Paris, in 1890. Over the years he lovingly built a garden there – a work of art in itself. Diverting a tiny river, he created a pond and planted its banks with flowers and willow trees. He painted it obsessively until the end of his life.

ART SPOT *Monet's carpet of water lilies looks thick enough here to walk on! How did he change his brushstrokes to show patches of uncovered water?*

JAPANESE DREAM

It is easy to see Monet's love of Japanese style in his water garden, with its curved footbridge, water lilies and willows. In 1899, he painted 18 views of it, most looking from the same angle. The symmetrical arch of the bridge cuts across the scene, cropped at the sides of the canvas. Monet also closes off the background by avoiding a strip of sky – something unseen in traditional landscape paintings.

The Water-Lily Pond, 1899

Water Lilies, 1906

FACE DOWN

In his later *Water Lilies* paintings, Monet dispensed with a horizon-line altogether. Looking down on the floating plants and reflections of the sky and trees, he tipped a horizontal scene onto a vertical canvas. This boldly original way of composing a painting caught the attention of later abstract artists, including Jackson Pollock (see p.41). Without any sense of space or distance, it keeps our eyes locked on the picture's surface.

FLOWER POWER

Andy Warhol (1928–1987) did something similar to Monet in his *Flowers* (right). Although there are swishes of grass or stems, the flowers have no recognisable setting. Warhol took the images from a photography magazine and turned them into colourful prints and paintings. Like his fellow Pop Artist, Roy Lichtenstein (see p.33), Warhol was interested in modern mass production. In 1964 he exhibited 48 of his flower pictures in series, much as Monet had done before.

Flowers, Andy Warhol, 1964

WATER LILY WALLS

Monet had grand ideas for his water lilies. In 1914 he started a series of enormous pictures – too big to paint at an easel. He set up a special glass-roofed studio, with the canvases propped on wheeled bases so he could move them around. Here he painted more than 40 panels, destroying some and starting new ones time and time again.

WATERY WORLD

Monet called the paintings his *'Grandes Decorations'*. He intended them to surround the walls of a room and immerse the viewer in a watery world. It took a large brush and a lot of paint to create this

ART SPOT
Monet loved the way water acted like a mirror. Can you tell where the leaves end and the reflections in the pond begin in Morning, with Weeping Willows *(below)?*

Morning, with Weeping Willows, 1926

effect. Monet built up the images layer after layer, until he had woven an elaborate web of colour and texture.

LIMITLESS SCENE

Monet said he wanted to create 'the illusion of an endless whole'. To do this, he left out any sign of a horizon or shore. We can't tell how far the pond stretches or how close he was to the tree. When you're standing among these gigantic panels, it feels as if the water goes on forever.

Monet at work on his giant water lily panels in 1923

Monet's *Grandes Decorations* on view at the Orangerie Museum in Paris

PRIDE OF PLACE

Monet started these paintings during the First World War. When the war ended in 1918 he offered a selection to the French state. Not everyone liked the ageing Monet's work – he was suffering from cataracts in his eyes, and many blamed his blindness for the unclear images. But in 1927, eight panels were hung in the Orangerie Museum in Paris, and they haven't moved since. A six-year renovation, finished in 2006, happened around them!

DECORATIVE EFFECT

One of the first people to see Monet's *Grandes Decorations* was his friend and fellow artist Pierre Bonnard (1867–1947). Living close to Giverny, Bonnard would visit Monet to admire his garden and watch the giant panels take shape. Bonnard was overwhelmed when he stood among the water lilies. You can see the influence of Monet's colours and brushwork in paintings like *Landscape in the South* (below). In a similar way to Monet, Bonnard focused on decorative effect and wove his paint into eye-catching patterns.

Landscape in the South, Pierre Bonnard, c.1943

ALMOST ABSTRACT

Surface texture had always been important to Monet, and in his old age he brought more and more of it to his work. He slapped down paint in expressive strokes that almost hid the subject of the painting. His failing eyesight did affect the way he saw colour and his sense of space – but these mature pieces were experiments in style, too.

CLOUDED VISION

As cataracts clouded Monet's vision, he began to rely more on memory and feeling. His colour vision changed, and he had to choose his paints by reading the label on the tube and arranging them in order on his palette. In *The Artist's House, seen from the Rose Garden* (below), the blues and lilacs of his water lilies are gone.

Instead we see a mass of flaming reds and yellows. Through the wild, heavy brushstrokes it is difficult to pick out the shape of the house in the background.

TANGLE OF PAINT

Some of Monet's late works are so lacking in readable detail, they would almost look the same upside down. *The Japanese Bridge* (opposite, top) is a tangle of colourful brushstrokes that reflect the energy that went into making them. Monet never completely removed subject from his pictures, but in these expressive thatches of paint he was nudging open the door to abstract art. He wasn't painting directly from nature, but what he saw in his mind's eye.

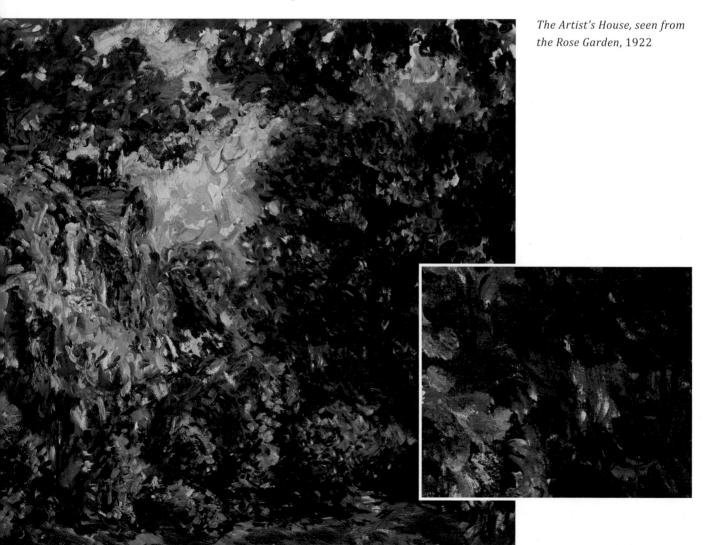

The Artist's House, seen from the Rose Garden, 1922

The Japanese Bridge,
1918–1924

GETTING PHYSICAL

Reflection of the Big Dipper, Jackson Pollock, 1946

The physical act of painting is clear in Monet's work – and the US artist Jackson Pollock (1912–1956) took this to extremes. He developed a style known as action painting, where he literally flung colours at a canvas on the floor! Pollock used liquid household paints and enamels instead of conventional oil paints. He poured, dribbled and splattered them until he built up a dense tapestry of marks (see right). This meant that much of his work was down to chance, though Pollock aimed his colours carefully and would often retouch drips with a brush.

ART SPOT *Jackson Pollock was known as an Abstract Expressionist. Can you work out what that means and why it applied to him? Can you identify similarities between this and Monet's work?*

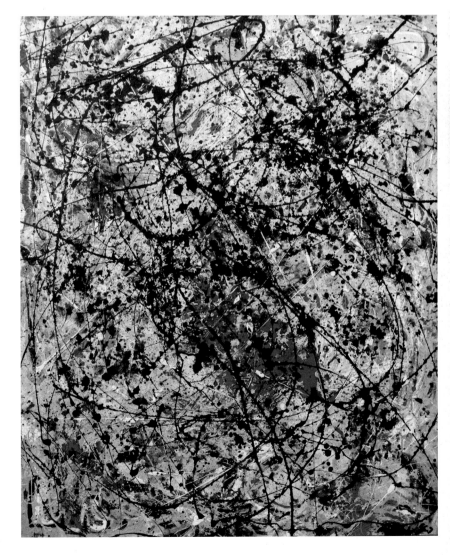

MONET-MANIA

Monet spent his final years working in virtual isolation at Giverny. He died in 1926, and was buried at the churchyard there. He had lived through rejection and great success, and though his reputation dipped in his later years, by the 1950s his work was making a comeback.

INFLUENCE IN AMERICA

In his lifetime, Monet inspired artists both in Europe and across the Atlantic. From 1887, a colony of American painters settled at Giverny to soak up their hero's surroundings. Many transmitted Monet's ideas back home. American Impressionists, such as Childe Hassam (1859–1935), started painting their own landscapes (opposite, top), influenced by Monet's style. The First World War brought the Giverny colony to an end, but Monet continued to work on paintings like the one below.

Water Lilies and Reflections of a Willow Tree, 1916–1919

Men o' War: 'The Blake' and 'The Boston',
Childe Hassam, 1893

CHANGING RECEPTION

In the early 20th century, Monet lost his limelight as other artists started finding new directions. Styles such as Cubism, Fauvism and Expressionism seemed more exciting and innovative. But when Abstract Expressionism rose up in the USA in the 1950s, Monet's art grabbed attention again. New exhibitions of his work caused a sensation. People could relate his mysterious images to the equally mysterious images of Jackson Pollock (see p.41) or Joan Mitchell (right).

LASTING IMPRESSION

These days, Monet's work is so popular you can even see it on mouse mats and iPad covers! It looks pretty and appealing – but that's not all it is. Monet turned the key to modern art when he showed that painting doesn't need a clear subject. He proved that colour and paint have a magic of their own and can change the way we see and feel about things. Many artists since have experimented with works in series or learnt from him in other ways. As the 20th-century painter André Masson once said, 'If there's a colourist alive today, he owes it to Monet, whether he knows it or not.'

La Grande Vallée XVI, Pour Iva, Joan Mitchell, 1983

TIMELINE

1840 Oscar-Claude Monet is born in Paris, France. He is later known as just Claude

1845 The family moves to Le Havre on the coast of Normandy, northwest France

1856 He meets Eugène Boudin and begins painting in the open air

1859 Monet moves to Paris to study art

1861 He starts his military service in Algeria, Africa

1862 Monet is sent home to recover from typhoid. Later that year he returns to Paris and enrols at a studio, where he befriends Pierre-Auguste Renoir and Alfred Sisley

1865 Monet paints outdoors with Renoir, Sisley and others. He meets Camille Doncieux

1866 Monet's *Woman in a Green Dress* is admired at the Salon. It sells for 800 francs – a lot of money in those days

1867 The Salon rejects *Women in the Garden*. Monet and Camille have their first child, Jean

1870 Monet marries Camille and they travel to England, via Trouville, to escape the Franco-Prussian War

1871 Monet visits the Netherlands, then settles in Argenteuil, northwest of Paris

1874 Monet and his group hold their first independent exhibition, which is ridiculed. They are nicknamed 'the Impressionists' based on the title of Monet's *Impression, Sunrise*

1876 Monet shows 18 pictures at the second Impressionist exhibition

1877 The third Impressionist exhibition includes 30 of Monet's works

1878 The Monets move to Vétheuil. Their second son, Michel is born. Camille's health declines and money is tight. They move in with Alice Hoschedé and family

1879 Monet shows 29 paintings at the fourth Impressionist show, and also exhibits at the Salon. Camille dies

1880 Monet does not take part in the fifth Impressionist exhibition, or the sixth in 1881

1881 Monet moves with Alice Hoschedé and all their children to Poissy, near Paris

1882 He exhibits with the Impressionists again at the seventh group exhibition

1883 Monet has a successful solo exhibition. He moves to Giverny, northwest of Paris

1886 He does not take part in the eighth and final Impressionist show

1890 Monet buys the house at Giverny where he will create his famous garden

1899 He visits London, returning again in 1900 and 1901

1908 He travels to Venice with Alice and paints

1915 Monet builds a huge new garden studio for his water lily panels

1923 He has a cataract operation, to try to correct one of his increasingly failing eyes. It is partially successful and he returns to work the following year

1926 Monet dies and is buried in Giverny, aged 86

1927 Eight of his water lily panels are installed at the Orangerie Museum, Paris and opened to the public

SELECTED WORKS

Background information on some
of Monet's works:

IMPRESSION, SUNRISE, 1872 (P.13)

When Monet painted *Impression, Sunrise*, he
had no idea it would name an art movement!
To him it was a fleeting glimpse of the port at
Le Havre, which he had known and loved since
his childhood. Monet knew he couldn't call it
a 'view' of Le Havre because critics would say
it was too sketchy. So he titled the painting
'Impression' – and was criticised even so!

Monet created this famous painting quickly,
probably in one sitting as he looked out from a
hotel window. Using swift strokes, he captured
the damp, grey air of a foggy morning with a
red rising sun burning through. We can see the
ghosts of ships' masts and chimneys on the
far-off quayside, with smaller boats silhouetted
up close. Monet tied the whole scene together
with delicate colours that link the sky with
reflections on the water.

THE GARE SAINT-LAZARE, 1877 (P.21)

At the time Monet was painting, the Gare
Saint-Lazare was the biggest, newest and
busiest train station in Paris. It was a dream
subject for an artist inspired by modern
engineering and the way it changed in different
conditions. You can imagine the thrill Monet got
from watching the light as it glinted through
the glass roof, reflected on shiny engines and
dissolved in clouds of steam.

The Gare Saint-Lazare contains plenty of the
Impressionists' favourite colour – violet.
It contrasts with the yellow tones of the distant
buildings and the station floor. With his thick
paint and bold brushstrokes, Monet created a
sense of sunlight swirling with dirty, smoky air.
The iron girders of the roof are broken by thick
puffs of steam, and the train workers and
travellers become little more than blobs as they
disappear down the platform.

THE SERIES PAINTINGS

Why did Monet paint so many haystacks?
Perhaps he saw them as a symbol of his local
landscape, or perhaps it was their shape that
appealed. Whatever his reasons, these conical
stacks of wheat aren't the most interesting
subject in themselves. But Monet made them
interesting by showing how much a solid,
motionless object can change. With the shift
of a shadow, the twinkle of snow, or the rising
or falling of the sun, he created a new image
every time.

You can see from the pictures on p.30–31 how
a viewpoint can make a difference too. Monet
sometimes moved around the haystacks,
lining them up in different ways. With Rouen
Cathedral (p.32–33) he was always up close
– but the nobbles and grooves in the walls
meant that the shadows constantly changed.
Variations like these are the secret to all of
Monet's series paintings. It's only when you
look from one picture to the next that the
impact really becomes clear.

WATER LILIES

Monet painted around 250 pictures of water
lilies! They occupied much of the last 30 years
of his life, when he'd declared he was 'good for
nothing except painting and gardening'. The
pinnacle came with his *Grandes Decorations*
(p.38–39), which together add up to over 90
metres in length. In them we see not just plants
on the water, but reflections of the sky, clouds
and leaves.

With his monumental water lily panels, Monet
changed the relationship between a painting
and its viewer. Usually when we look at a
picture of a landscape or seascape, we are
bigger than the view that's on the canvas. But
standing amid Monet's *Grandes Decorations*,
we come face to face with a vast and seemingly
endless expanse of water. Showing a sky or
water's edge would normally help to put the
scene in context. Monet chose to leave these
features out.

abstract not representing an actual object, place or living thing. Abstract art often focusses on basic shapes, lines, colours or use of space

Abstract Expressionism an American style (1940s–1950s) in which artists aimed to create abstract art with an emotional effect. Action painting (p.41) was one type of Abstract Expressionism. The other was Colour-field painting, where artists painted large patches of colour to provoke a response in the viewer

boulevard a wide street or avenue

canvas a strong type of fabric that many artists use to paint on, especially in oils

caricature a humorous portrait drawing where certain features or characteristics are exaggerated

cataract a clouding of the lens in the eye, causing loss of vision

complementary colours colours that have maximum contrast between each other. The basic pairs for artists are red and green, blue and orange, and yellow and purple

composition the way parts of a picture are arranged

contemporary living in our time – or the same time as someone else. (Monet's contemporaries included Pierre-Auguste Renoir and Paul Cézanne)

Cubism an art style (1907–1920s) in which artists, led by Pablo Picasso and Georges Braque,

made images using simplified shapes and multiple viewpoints

Divisionism also known as Pointillism – the technique of painting using small, regular dots of unmixed colour. Georges Seurat pioneered the idea, based on scientific theories about complementary colours and their relationships to one another.

easel a wooden stand that supports an artist's canvas or drawing board

ethereal relating to the air or sky; otherworldly

Expressionism an art style (1905–1920s) in which artists tried to convey different emotions, often through exaggerated colours or distorted shapes

Fauve belonging to the art style Fauvism (c.1905–1910) in which artists such as Henri Matisse and André Derain used extreme colours and striking brushstrokes

foreground the part of a scene that's nearest to the viewer

geometric based on mathematical shapes such as the triangle, circle or sphere

impasto using paint thickly so that it stands out from the picture surface

Impressionism an art style (c.1874–1886) in which artists such as Claude Monet painted mostly outdoors, capturing fleeting moments using vivid colours and dappled brushstrokes

Neo-Impressionist the name given to Georges Seurat and his followers, who developed the style Divisionism (see above) in the 1880s

palette a board that artists mix their colours on. The word is also used to describe the range of colours in a painting

perspective the art of showing three-dimensional objects on a flat surface, creating the effect of depth or distance. Linear perspective involves a vanishing point on the horizon that everything leads towards

pigment a type of colouring, usually in powdered form, that forms the basis of paint

Pop Art a UK and US art style (1950s–1960s) that celebrated the bold, brash images of advertising and modern mass production

Pop Art a UK and US art style (1950s–1960s) that celebrated the bold, brash images of advertising and modern mass production

print a way of transferring an image from one surface to another, by covering a raised or engraved design with paint or ink and pressing it onto paper

Salon an official art exhibition in Paris, held yearly or twice yearly from 1737. It favoured traditional artists of the time, but was later joined by more progressive rivals such as the Salon d'Automne

spontaneous done suddenly or without much forethought

studio an artist's indoor workplace

suburb a residential area on the outskirts of a city

synthetic artificially or chemically made, usually to imitate a natural product

texture the feel of a surface, such as rough brick or smooth glass

typhoid an infectious disease, caused by bacteria in contaminated food or water

vibrant bright and lively

INDEX

FURTHER INFORMATION

BOOKS:

Great Artists of the World: Claude Monet by Alix Wood (Franklin Watts, 2015)
Impressionism: 13 Artists Children Should Know by Florian Heine, (Prestel, 2015)
Monet: Masters of Art by Simona Bartolena (Prestel, 2014)

WEBSITES:

Learn about Monet and his paintings at London's National Gallery:
www.nationalgallery.org.uk/artists/claude-monet
Watch a slideshow of 48 of Monet's paintings:
www.bbc.co.uk/arts/yourpaintings/artists/claude-monet
Read an overview of Monet's life:
www.biography.com/people/claude-monet-9411771#the-master-of-light-and-color
Explore Monet's Grandes Decorations at the Orangerie Musuem:
www.musee-orangerie.fr